DR HELEN KENNERLEY qualified in Clinical Psychology in Oxford, where she also trained to become a cognitive therapist. She is one of the founder members of the Oxford Cognitive Therapy Centre (OCTC). Currently, she works as a consultant within OCTC, where she is the lead clinician of a specialist clinic in cognitive therapy. Helen has presented many workshops pertaining to her areas of clinical expertise both nationally and internationally. In 2002 she was shortlisted by the British Association for Behavioural and Cognitive Psychotherapies for the award for most influential female cognitive therapist in Britain.

The Overcoming series was initiated by PETER COOPER, Professor of Psychology at the University of Reading and Honorary NHS Consultant Clinical Psychologist. His original book on bulimia nervosa and binge-eating founded the series in 1993 and continues to help many thousands of people in the USA, the UK and Europe. The aim of the series is to help people with a wide range of common problems and disorders to take control of their own recovery programme using the latest techniques of cognitive behavioural therapy. Each book, with its specially tailored programme, is devised by a practising clinician. Many books in the Overcoming series are now recommended by the UK Department of Health under the Books on Prescription scheme.

Other titles in the Overcoming series:

3-part self-help courses

Overcoming Low Self-Esteem Self-Help Course
Overcoming Bulimia Nervosa and Binge-Eating Self-Help Course

Single volume books

Overcoming Anger and Irritability
Overcoming Anorexia Nervosa
Overcoming Anxiety
Bulimia Nervosa and Binge-Eating
Overcoming Childhood Trauma
Overcoming Chronic Fatigue
Overcoming Chronic Pain
Overcoming Compulsive Gambling
Overcoming Depression
Overcoming Insomnia and Sleep Problems
Overcoming Low Self-Esteem
Overcoming Mood Swings
Overcoming Obsessive Compulsive Disorder
Overcoming Panic
Overcoming Relationship Problems
Overcoming Sexual Problems
Overcoming Social Anxiety and Shyness
Overcoming Traumatic Stress
Overcoming Weight Problems
Overcoming Your Smoking Habit

Contents

Note to Practitioners

This self-help course is suitable for a wide range of reading abilities and its step-by-step format makes it ideal for working through alone or under supervision. The course is divided into three workbooks, and each contains a full supply of worksheets and charts to be filled in on the page – so there is no need for photocopying. If you do decide to photocopy this material you will need to seek the permission of the publishers to avoid a breach of copyright law.

Introduction: How to Use this Workbook

This is a self-help course for dealing with problem worries, fears and anxieties. It has two aims:

1 To help you develop a better understanding of the problem

2 To teach you some practical coping skills

How the course works

The *Overcoming Anxiety Self-Help Course* will help you understand how anxiety develops and what keeps it going, and then to make changes in your life so that you begin to feel more confident.

These workbooks are designed to help you work, either by yourself or with your healthcare practitioner, to overcome anxiety. With plenty of questionnaires, charts, worksheets and practical exercises, the three parts together make up a structured course.

Part One explained the origins and development of problem worries, fears and anxieties. You learnt:

- What anxiety and stress are

- Whether you have a problem with anxiety

- What the difference is between helpful short-term anxiety and unhelpful long-term anxiety

- Why anxiety has become a problem for you

- The cycles that maintain and worsen your anxiety

- What kind of anxiety disorder you might be suffering from

Part Two explains:

- How to ease the physical sensations of anxiety through controlled breathing and relaxation techniques

- How to deal with worrying thoughts

- How to face your fears using planning and problem-solving

Part Three gives advice on:

- Assertiveness training to help you handle relationships better

- Time management to help you improve decision-making and your organizational skills

- Sleep management to help you get a better night's rest

- Guidance for coping with anxiety in the long term

How long will the course take?

Although it will vary from person to person, it will probably take you at least two or three weeks to work through each workbook. You should not worry if you feel that you need to give certain parts extra time. Some things can be understood or practised quite quickly, but others may take longer. You will know when you are ready to move on to the next workbook. Completing the entire course could take two to three months, or it could take more or less time – it depends how quickly you wish to work.

Getting the most from the course

Here are some tips to help you get the most from the workbooks:

- These workbooks are not priceless antiques – they are practical tools. So feel free not only to write on the worksheets and charts, but also to underline and highlight things, and to write comments and questions in the margins. By the time you have finished with a workbook, it should look well and truly used.

- You will also find lots of space in the main text. These are for you to write down your thoughts and ideas, and your responses to the questions.

- Keep an open mind and be willing to experiment with new ideas and skills. These books will sometimes ask you to think about painful issues. However, if anxiety is distressing you and restricting your life, it really is worth making the effort to overcome it. The rewards will be substantial.

- Be prepared to invest time in doing the practical exercises – set aside 20 to 30 minutes each day if you can. You can maintain your achievements by practising your coping skills regularly and knowing how to learn from setbacks.

- Try to answer all the questions and do the exercises, even if you have to come back to some of them later. There may be times when you get stuck and can't think how to take things forward. If this happens, don't get angry with yourself or give up. Just put the book aside and come back to it later, when you are feeling more relaxed.

- You may find it helpful to work through the books with a friend. Two heads are often better than one. And you may be able to encourage each other to persist, even when one of you is finding it hard. Ask for the help of family and friends, particularly in the practical tasks.

- Re-read the workbook. You may get more out of it once you've had a chance to think about some of the ideas and put them into practice for a little while.

- Each workbook builds on what has already been covered. So what you learn when working with one will help you when you come to the next. It's quite possible simply to dip into different ones as you please, but you may get most out of the series if you follow them through systematically, step by step.

What if I don't feel better?

There is nothing to lose by working through this book; it will give you practical coping skills you can put into practice straight away. However, if you find that self-help alone is not meeting your needs (this is sometimes the case), see your family doctor, medical practitioner or specialist therapist, who can offer extra support. If you do need to seek more help this doesn't mean you have failed in any way; just that your difficulties are perhaps more complex.

A note of caution

These workbooks will not help everyone who has problem worries, fears and anxieties. If you find that focusing on anxiety is actually making you feel worse instead of better, you may be suffering from clinical depression. The recognized signs of clinical depression include:

- Constantly feeling sad, down, depressed or empty

- General lack of interest in what's going on around you

- A big increase or decrease in your appetite and weight

- A marked change in your sleep patterns

- Noticeable speeding up or slowing down in your movements and how you go about things

- Feeling of being tired and low in energy

- An intense sense of guilt or worthlessness

- Difficulty in concentrating and making decisions

- A desire to hurt yourself or a feeling that you might be better off dead

If you have had five or more of these symptoms (including low mood or loss of interest) for two weeks or more, you should seek professional help from a doctor, counsellor or psychotherapist. There is nothing shameful about seeking this sort of professional help – any more than there is anything shameful about taking your car to a garage if it is not working as it should, or going to see a lawyer if you have legal problems. It simply means taking your journey towards self-knowledge and self-acceptance with the help of a friendly guide, rather than striking out alone.

SECTION 1: Building a First Aid Kit

In Part Two you will learn about:

- Awareness training and self-monitoring
- Breathing control techniques
- Relaxation techniques
- Distraction
- Challenging worrying thoughts and images

With these strategies and techniques together with others you will learn in Part Three you can begin to take control of your problem. However, you should remember that coping strategies rarely come naturally. You need to think of them as *skills* that can only be learned through regular practice. Developing these skills is like learning to play a musical instrument – you have to find time to practise and be prepared for some of the work to be hard or tedious. With practice, you will find that you can call on effective coping strategies whenever you are under stress or feeling anxious.

As you work through the exercises and strategies, ask yourself the following questions.

Do any of the strategies seem familiar?

Some of the strategies you will learn about may be similar to coping techniques that you have tried already, but which haven't worked. Don't dismiss them as you can often build on your current coping methods. Read through the sections carefully and check that you have been using the technique properly. If a particular technique was not helpful to you in the past, also think about whether or not you have been practising it enough.

Which strategies are new to you?

Some of the strategies will be quite new to you. Don't be put off – some of these might prove to be the most effective ones for you. However, do recognize that the unfamiliar strategies are likely to need extra attention and practice.

Which strategies 'match' your problem best?

As a general guide, look for coping strategies that 'match' your problems. For example, if you suffer from the physical discomfort of stress, make sure that controlled breathing and relaxation are on your list of skills. If you are more bothered by constant worries and nagging fears, invest extra time in learning distraction techniques and how to challenge worrying thoughts. The best way to match strategies to your needs will be covered in more detail later.

Which strategies fit best into your life?

You need to develop coping strategies that fit in with your lifestyle. For instance, it's not realistic to overcome a fear of flying by enlisting for flying lessons if you don't have the finances, or to visit a gym for relaxation if you have small children and no childcare. But you could make plans that involve the support of others if you have helpful family and friends, or take time off work if you have sympathetic employers. In Section 2 you will discover how keeping a diary can help you to identify your personal needs and resources.

Do you prefer learning to cope on your own, or by getting the support of your partner, family or friends?

Although this is a self-help guide, you can ask others for support if this will improve your stress management. Partners, family and friends can be great allies in coping, and so can professionals such as counsellors or doctors.

Make a list of family, friends, professionals, etc. who could form part of your support team.

_____

_____

_____

_____

_____

_____

_____

_____

_____

_____

_____

_____

As you work through the exercises, think about if and where you need to call in support. Return to this list and consider who is best suited to help you with which task.

What do you expect from this self-help programme?

It's important to think about what you personally expect to get out of these manuals. Are you simply looking for day-to-day relief from some of the symptoms of your problem, or do you hope to take full control of it? Are there particular symptoms you want to get on top of (for example, troubled sleep, rapid breathing, distressing thoughts), or do you have specific goals (for example, flying abroad for the first time, or giving a best man's speech at a wedding)? Perhaps your goals are more general (for example, an end to panic attacks or come off anti-anxiety drugs)?

What are your goals and targets? Write down your expectations and hopes for the self-help programme. Try to be specific if you can as it is much easier to plan interventions and monitor progress if your goals are tangible.

_____

_____

_____

_____

Do you feel that you need more help managing your problem?

Ultimately you may hope to gain full control of your anxiety, but for some people self-help will only get them so far. The strategies in these manuals can help on every level, but you may find you need additional support. Don't be dismayed; simply contact a professional, such as your family doctor, who can advise you where to go for further help.

Tranquillizers

In the 1970s and early 1980s medication – in particular, tranquillizers – was a popular way to cope with anxiety. Tranquillizers are not necessarily bad things as long as they are used under the advice of a doctor. In fact they can be very helpful for someone in a crisis; but in the long term they can sometimes cause problems. These include:

- Becoming physically dependent on them
- Allowing you to avoid your problem so you become psychologically dependent on them as a coping strategy
- Masking the symptoms of anxiety but not helping you deal with the root of the problem
- Unpleasant side effects which can worsen anxiety

By contrast there is good evidence that self-help can be effective for anxiety problems without the above disadvantages. However, for a self-help programme to work, it is important that:

- It is organized in a way that helps you pace yourself realistically
- The techniques used in the self-help programme are practised regularly and that you understand them

Coming off medication

If you are already using tranquillizers, the best way to come off them is to learn self-help skills to replace them. However, before changing your medication, it is important to talk this through with your doctor. He or she can advise on the best rate of reduction and monitor the withdrawal effects that some people suffer. Withdrawal effects may include:

- feelings of anxiety
- loss of concentration and poor memory

- agitation and restlessness

- stomach upsets

- sensitivity to light and noise

- feelings of unreality (for example, as though you are watching a movie of your life)

- physical tension and pain

- appetite changes

- sleep problems.

Not everyone will experience these symptoms, so don't *expect* to suffer as you cut back on your drugs.

If you *do* experience symptoms of withdrawal, discuss them with your doctor and reassure yourself that they are usually temporary and that your body and mind will adjust. Try not to use alcohol, caffeine, food or cigarettes as substitutes/comforters, as these bring their own problems (see Part One, page 22). Instead, use the self-help strategies outlined in this manual and in Part Three.

When it comes to your medication, you and your doctor should be partners in determining and directing your treatment. Filling in the chart on the next page can help you to get perspective on your drug use, identify points for discussion with your doctor and, thus, become active in your therapy.

- In column 1 make a list of medication that you take to help with anxiety.

- In column 2 list the side effects that you feel are associated with each medication.

- Briefly note your goals with respect to that medication – would you like to be able to come off it or simply cut down?

- Set intermediate goals, with a target time frame – for example, to reduce use with one month, and stop entirely within three. Goals and targets should not be too ambitious, and must include a commitment to developing alternative, non-drug coping strategies.

- Use the chart next time you speak to your doctor, as a basis for discussion and planning.

Medication (dosage)	Unpleasant physical/mental experiences

My goals

Intermediate goals

Summary

1   These workbooks will help you discover which techniques will help you cope best with anxiety.

2   Each person's 'kit' will be different and it is important that you tailor yours to meet your needs, by reflecting on your particular lifestyle and resources.

3   Self-help can help you reduce the use of tranquillizers but always discuss this with your doctor first.

SECTION 2: Awareness Training and Self-monitoring

The experience of worry, fear and anxiety is different for each of us. We do not all experience the same physical symptoms: each of us has our own worrying thoughts, we each behave differently and the triggers for anxieties vary from person to person. Before you can manage your anxiety problem you must really understand it.

The best way to do this is by keeping a record of times when you are particularly worried, fearful or anxious. At those times, write down your physical feelings, your thoughts and what you do when you feel this distress.

This section shows you how to keep an anxiety diary. But first, read about how Alison found her anxiety diary helped her.

CASE STUDY: Alison

'For a long time I thought that my panic came out of the blue. This made me even more frightened because I felt out of control. Then I started to keep a diary of my panicky feelings and, to my surprise, I saw a pattern. This made me feel less helpless and I started to re-organize my life to minimize the panics. For example, I got the feelings if I hadn't eaten for hours, so I began to carry snacks in my briefcase. I felt panicky when I had to see my boss, so I joined an assertiveness training class to help me feel more confident around her. My diary helped me take control again.'

Keeping an anxiety diary

Diary 1 shows the record of Anne, who has a phobia of dogs. Diaries 2 and 3 show the records of Barbara who suffers from social anxiety and Chris who suffers from obsessive-compulsive disorder. On pages 70–77 you will find blank diary forms for you to fill in.

DIARY 1: Dog Phobia

Monitor your stress levels each day, noting when you feel particularly worried, frightened or anxious. Use the diary as near to the time of distress as possible as it is easy to forget the details later. Record the occasion and rate the severity of your feelings (1–10). Where you can, note what triggered the stress – thoughts, images, feelings, events, for example. Also, record how you tried to cope, and afterwards, rerate your distress levels.

Rate your distress on the following scale:

1	2	3	4	5	6	7	8	9	10
No distress, calm				Moderate distress					Absolute panic

Date/time	What was the occasion?	Rating	What brought it on?	How did you try to cope?	Rerating
Saturday, 12.30pm	Waiting for Jim & Sue to arrive for our trip out for a drink	8	Worry that I'd see a dog at the bar and I'd go to pieces	1. Tried to do something else: read a magazine	6
1.00pm	In their car, on the way to the bar	8	Ditto	2. Tried something more distracting: rang Mary to talk about work.	4
1.20pm	Sitting outside bar waiting for Jim to bring over the drinks	10	I saw a shape in the parkland – I was sure it was a dog – probably a German Shepherd	Kept talking to Sue to take my mind off the worries.	6
				1. Screamed. Then Sue told me that it was a small deer, not a dog.	8
				2. Drank 2 glasses of wine quickly!	4
				3. Went inside bar	3
3.00pm	At home, alone. The alcohol is wearing off.	7	Remember the stress and the fright of today	Try to relax in the garden with classical music on my personal stereo	2

DIARY 2: Social Anxiety

Monitor your stress levels each day, noting when you feel particularly worried, frightened or anxious. Use the diary as near to the time of distress as possible as it is easy to forget the details later. Record the occasion and rate the severity of your feelings (1–10). Where you can, note what triggered the stress – thoughts, images, feelings, events, for example. Also, record how you tried to cope, and afterwards, rerate your distress levels.

Rate your distress on the following scale:

1	2	3	4	5	6	7	8	9	10
No distress, calm				Moderate distress					Absolute panic

Date/time	What was the occasion?	Rating	What brought it on?	How did you try to cope?	Rerating
Monday, 10.00am	First day back at college. In the college lodge – David suggests I join him and some friends for lunch later on.	8	Panic! I can't face students that I don't know. I won't be able to join in the conversation – they'll think I'm stupid. I am stupid!	Declined the offer.	3
10.30am	First lecture: sitting at the back on my own – thinking about David.	6	Misery – I'm such a wimp – pathetic. I'll never get confident this way.	Left David a note to suggest lunch at my place tomorrow with just two of my friends.	2
Friday 11.00pm	At Tony's party in the student common room. About 50 students.	8	Anxiety. I don't know anyone. I dare not approach anyone and no one is going to approach me. I am a failure.	Made my excuses to leave early and sat in my room brooding for two hours.	3
					8
Saturday 12.00am	In town – saw a group of students from last night's party.	8	Panic! They'll see me and recognize me as the wimp from the party. I am such a fool – I should have stayed.	Hid in the bookshop until they'd gone past. Went back to college quickly.	6

DIARY 3: Obsessive-Compulsive Disorder

Monitor your stress levels each day, noting when you feel particularly worried, frightened or anxious. Use the diary as near to the time of distress as possible as it is easy to forget the details later. Record the occasion and rate the severity of your feelings (1–10). Where you can, note what triggered the stress – thoughts, images, feelings, events, for example. Also, record how you tried to cope, and afterwards, rerate your distress levels.

Rate your distress on the following scale:

1	2	3	4	5	6	7	8	9	10
No distress, calm				Moderate distress				Absolute panic	

Date/time	What was the occasion?	Rating	What brought it on?	How did you try to cope?	Rerating
Tuesday, 3.00pm	Heard about car crash on the news. Whole family killed.	9	Picture in my mind of the pile-up and my family being involved.	Kept repeating my 'lucky' words and repeatedly phoned home to check that they were ok. No answer so kept phoning for 2 hours.	8
Thursday 10.00pm	Reading the newspaper: story about cars catching fire because of faulty electrics.	9	Saw myself in burning car and remembered that I should have had our car serviced by now.	Shut the newspaper and didn't finish reading the story. Tried to forget. Repeated 'lucky' words over and over.	9
Saturday 3.30pm	Driving with Rosie when we went past a road traffic accident.	9	Saw myself in the car crash. Thought 'it's my own fault because you've not had the car serviced.'	Talked through my fears which helped me see that they were exaggerated. Booked a car service.	3

The diary has the following columns:

- **Date and time.** Recording the date and time might help you find a pattern; for example, perhaps your anxiety worse in the mornings or when you haven't had enough to eat. Record episodes as near to the time of distress as possible, as it is easy to forget the details later.

- **What was the occasion?** Be specific and include any possibly relevant details.

- **Rating.** Use this column to give a rating of the severity of your anxiety. Rate your distress on the following scale:

1	2	3	4	5	6	7	8	9	10
No distress, calm				Moderate distress			The worst that I can imagine		

- **What brought it on?** If possible record what triggered the stress, including any relevant thoughts, images, feelings or events.

- **How did you try to cope?** Record what you did as a result of the anxiety, whether or not it was helpful. Don't limit yourself to one thing. This column might reflect what you do intuitively or specific techniques that you are trying out.

- **Rerating.** Use the same scale to rate your anxiety levels after you've taken whatever steps/measures you described in the previous column. This will help you to work out whether your coping strategies are working or not.

- **What have I learnt?** Reflect on what your experience tells you. You might have learnt more about your personal strengths and needs and how you might use this in the future (e.g: 'I have learnt that can talk myself through a panic attack if I intervene early enough. In future, I will make time for self-talk instead of trying to press on.')

Record your experiences with anxiety for two weeks, using the blank diary sheets on pages 70–77. Once they are filled in, you will be able to answer these important questions:

- What things or situations trigger my distress?

- What are my physical feelings and my thoughts when I am distressed?

- Do different situations cause different levels of stress?

- What do I tend to do when I'm distressed?

- What helps me best to cope with my distress?

The last question is particularly important. It's important to find out which coping strategies help and are good for you in the long run. You will also discover the strategies which might make you feel better in the short term but are not helpful over time.

Using your diaries 1: Getting to know your coping skills

'Short-term only' coping strategies

Strategies that are 'short-term only' are those measures that provide only temporary, short-lived relief. They are often unhelpful in the long run – for example using tranquillizers or alcohol, avoiding difficult situations or scolding yourself. These responses are likely to erode self-confidence in the long term; however, 'short-term only' strategies can be useful if they give you a bit of breathing space: time to put into action long-term strategies. They can also be useful as a last resort, when you've run out of other options.

CASE STUDY: Bette

'I began to get out more when I learnt to keep my mind off my social worries by always keeping busy: handing round the drinks, helping with the washing up, always being the one to volunteer to go and fetch things. Gradually I realized that this was not helping me build up my self-confidence because I was actually still avoiding mixing socially. Bit by bit, I've made myself engage in conversations and mix with people, and this is really helping me grow less anxious. However, if I have to 'psych' myself up in a social situation, I still use keeping busy just to buy me some time to get my thinking straight. Recently I was surprised and overwhelmed by the size of my friend's birthday party and I did use the 'busy-strategy' quite a lot because I really wanted to be able to be there for her that night.'

Use the sample diaries to identify the 'short-term only' strategies used by Anne, Barbara and Chris. Record your findings in the chart below. We have started each one for you.

Which strategies helped them the most (i.e. produced the biggest drop in 'Anxiety Rating' on rerating)? You can use the sample ratings to put an actual figure on this – simply subtract the rerating from the first rating.

	'Short-term only' coping strategies	**Drop in anxiety rating**
Anne	Moved inside bar to get away from perceived threat of a dog	7
Barbara	Turned down invitation	5
Chris	Performed obsessive routine; attempted to phone family	1

Now use your own diaries to make a record of your own short-term coping strategies.

	'Short-term only' coping strategies	**Drop in anxiety rating**
1		
2		
3		
4		
5		
6		
7		
8		
9		
10		

Long-term strategies

Long-term coping strategies are those that are helpful in both the short and long term – those that help you to gain more permanent control of your anxiety. These include using relaxation exercises, physically facing your fear and problem-solving.

Their impact might not be as immediate as some of the 'short-term only' strategies, so you sometimes need more patience, self-discipline or bravery to put them into action.

Use the sample diaries to identify the long-term strategies used by Anne, Barbara and Chris. Again, work out which ones helped the most.

	Long-term coping strategies	Drop in anxiety rating
Anne	Relaxed in garden with classical music	5
Barbara	Arranged small gathering – not too taxing	4
Chris	Talked through fears with partner	6

Now use your own diaries to make a record of your own long-term coping strategies.

	Long-term coping strategies	Drop in anxiety rating
1		
2		
3		
4		
5		
6		
7		
8		
9		
10		

Moving from short- to long-term strategies

Don't feel that you have to give up all your 'short-term' coping strategies at once: this can be frightening. Instead, think how you might begin to introduce more helpful coping strategies into your collection of techniques.

Caffeine, nicotine and alcohol

When you are trying to cope, it is especially important to try not to turn to substances such as alcohol and nicotine, or caffeine-containing food and drink such as chocolate, chocolate drinks, coffee, cola drinks or tea. In the short term these can provide a pleasant distraction from your problem; but as soon as the caffeine or nicotine enters your system, they will increase the unpleasant physical symptoms and make managing your stress more difficult. Alcohol is deceptive, in that it *is* relaxing in the short term. However, the breakdown products of alcohol are stimulants, so you can find yourself more tense than ever once the alcohol has been processed by your body. Heavy drinking will cause a hangover, which will simply add to your stress and using alcohol is often a form of avoidance which will undermine progress. Try to acquire a taste for decaffeinated or non-caffeinated drinks and foods, and try to cut back on smoking and drinking alcohol when you are stressed.

Using your diaries 2: Identify your maintaining cycles

When you have kept a diary of stress for a short while, you will discover the form your problem takes and how you tend to deal with it. Study your diary, with the help of the following exercises, and you should be able to work out the cycles that maintain it. Before tackling this section, you may find it helpful to go back to Part One and review the section on 'How anxiety works'.

Practise your skills

Before attempting to tease out your own maintaining cycles, review your knowledge of how they work by practising on the sample diaries of Anne, Barbara and Chris shown earlier. The table on the next page lists the types of physical, psychological, emotional, behavioural and social maintaining cycles that were introduced in Part One.

1 Use the list of maintaining cycles to review the sample diaries.

2 For each episode listed, ask yourself which cycles were at work?

3 Fill in your answers in the table opposite, and then check with the answer table on page 18.

4 Remember, there may be more than one maintaining cycle working at the same time.

Maintaining cycles

Physical cycles

Sweating

Breathlessness

Racing heart

Stomach problems

Psychological cycles

Fear of fear – feeling anxious about the symptoms of anxiety

Self-fulfilling prophecies about behaviour

Catastrophizing – expecting the worst

All-or-nothing thinking

Exaggerating

Jumping to conclusions

Over-generalizing

Scanning – looking out for the thing that makes you anxious

Ignoring the positive – not hearing compliments, 'good news', etc.

Worrying

Emotional cycles

Mood changes

Behavioural cycles

Avoidance/escape – escaping or running away from the anxiety

Reassurance seeking

Social cycles

Life events – stressful events over which you have no control

Other people – both obvious 'negative' people and those people who are well intentioned

	What was happening	Maintaining cycles at work
Anne	Waiting to go to bar	
	In car on way to bar	
	Sitting outside bar	
	At home at end of day	
Barbara	Invited to small party	
	Thinking about David	
	Party in the common room	
	Encounter students in town	
Chris	Heard news item	
	Read news item	
	Drove past accident	

Answers:

	Episode	Maintaining cycles at work
Anne	Waiting to go to bar	Fear of fear; catastrophizing; avoidance
	In car on way to bar	Fear of fear; catastrophizing; avoidance
	Sitting outside bar	Scanning; jumping to conclusions; avoidance; escape
	At home at end of day	Ignoring the positive; bodily distress
Barbara	Invited to small party	Bodily distress; catastrophizing; all-or-nothing thinking; ignoring the positive; avoidance
	Thinking about David	Catastrophizing; all-or-nothing thinking; ignoring the positive; over-generalization
	Party in the common room	Mood changes; catastrophizing; all-or-nothing thinking; escape; exaggerating
	Encounter students in town	Bodily distress; exaggerating; escape
Chris	Heard news item	Catastrophizing; over-generalization; avoidance; reassurance seeking
	Read news item	Scanning; catastrophizing; over-generalization; avoidance
	Drove past accident	Life event; catastrophizing; over-generalization

How did you do? If you struggled with this exercise, you may need to review the material in Part One.

Analyse your own maintaining cycles

Now analyse your own anxiety diaries. Fill in the table below.

Episode	Maintaining cycles at work

Creating the best personal programme

Now you can use these findings to target your development of coping strategies. Make sure to include the ones best suited to tackling your individual pattern of anxiety.

- If **physical discomfort** is keeping your anxiety going, focus on the techniques for managing physical symptoms.

- If **worrying thoughts** are your main source of stress, learn the techniques of distraction and thought challenging.

- If you **avoid problems** and **lack confidence,** focus on a programme of facing your fears (see Part Three).

- If you find **relationships stressful,** focus on assertiveness training (see Part Three).

The coping strategies in this book are laid out so as to make it easy for you to focus on particular areas. The table below will help you to decide which strategies will be most useful to you. It is a good idea to try all of the strategies. You might need to use more than one strategy to tackle a problem. Remember, as well, that we each have different needs and strengths. Adapt the self-help programme to meet your needs and goals.

Coping strategy	When should I give this special attention?
Self-monitoring, diary-keeping	Throughout your programme. This will help you to build up an accurate picture of your needs and will also provide a record of your progress.
Techniques for managing physical sensations	
Controlled breathing	If you experience panic attacks, difficulty in breathing, dizziness. It is also a good idea to learn this as part of your relaxation training.
Applied relaxation	If you have much physical tension or bodily discomfort when you are stressed. This can also be very helpful with sleep problems.

Coping strategy	When should I give this special attention?
Techniques for managing psychological symptoms	
Distraction	If you have difficulty dismissing worries and upsetting mental images. This can also be very useful in panic management.
Thought challenging	If you need a powerful and long-lasting form of self-reassurance, thought challenging can help you manage the problem in both the short and long term.
Techniques for dealing with problem behaviours	
Graded exposure to fears	If you avoid what you fear, you *must* learn to face the fear.
Problem-solving strategies	If you have difficulty organizing your thoughts and making plans when you are under stress.
Assertiveness training	If inter-personal problems stress you.
Time management	If your stress management is undermined by poor organization or delegation.
Sleep management	If you are not getting enough sleep or worry about sleeping properly.
Techniques for coping in the long term	
Blueprinting	This is an essential part of the programme for all users.
Coping with setbacks	This is essential and should be given attention throughout the programme.

Summary

1 In order to manage your worries, fears and anxieties, you need to monitor them and become familiar with their triggers and the sensations, thoughts and behaviour which they cause. You can do this through keeping a diary.

2 You also need to identify your current coping methods so that you can turn the useful ones to your best advantage, while limiting your use of the less helpful ones. Again, you can do this through diary keeping.

3 In order to manage your problems you will have to work through the entire self-help programme.

4 You can use your records of *your* stress responses to identify *your* special needs. You should then match these with the different elements of the recovery programme so that you can see which aspects of the programme *you* should emphasize.

SECTION 3: Learning to Control Your Breathing

Breathing comes naturally and we can all do it. However, there is a comfortable and an uncomfortable way to breathe. The uncomfortable way is rapid and shallow breathing when we are not exerting ourselves. This uses only the upper part of the lungs and results in taking in too much oxygen, unless we use up that oxygen through vigorous activity. This is the sort of breathing that you will find yourself doing after you have just run to catch a bus. This rapid breathing is a perfectly normal response to exertion and stress and is called overbreathing or *hyperventilation*. In the short term overbreathing is not a problem. However, if you continue to overbreathe, without using up the excess oxygen, you will feel physical discomfort.

In this section, you will learn a simple breathing exercise to overcome hyperventilation and help you relax.

Hyperventilation

We all hyperventilate whenever we are tense or when we are exercising.

- Rapid breathing allows you to take in more air and therefore more oxygen.
- This gives your muscles more oxygen to burn, allowing them to perform at a higher rate or recover from exertion more quickly.
- During periods of stress, this means that your body is better equipped for fight-or-flight (see Part One).

Continued hyperventilation, however, can cause unpleasant physical and mental effects. Work through the checklist below and tick any symptoms that you have experienced when you were anxious.

☐ Tingling face, hands or limbs   ☐ Unable to catch breath

☐ Muscle tremors   ☐ Feeling of suffocation

☐ Cramps   ☐ Exhaustion/fatigue

☐ Dizziness   ☐ Chest pains

☐ Light-headedness   ☐ Stomach pains

☐ Spots before eyes   ☐ Panic

☐ Tunnel vision   ☐ Feeling of loss of control

☐ Blurred vision   ☐ Fear that you may pass out/collapse

If you have ticked several boxes you may suffer from unhelpful hyperventilation.

How hyperventilation can worsen anxiety and panic

Hyperventilation causes an increased amount of oxygen to get into your blood-stream. This disrupts the normal balance of oxygen and carbon dioxide in your blood. It is this imbalance which triggers the unpleasant physical symptoms which can be very powerful – it is not unusual for extreme sufferers to presume that they are having a heart attack or a stroke, for example.

These symptoms are distressing in themselves and cause further alarm, which further worsens your stress levels. This in turn can lead to more stress-related hyperventilation. A vicious cycle can emerge: hyperventilation-related symptoms trigger alarming thoughts, such as feeling that you are losing control or about to pass out, and these heighten anxiety which promotes further hyperventilation.

Read Alex's story below and underline anything you relate to.

CASE STUDY: Alex – Part 1

Alex suffers from a phobia of birds. One day, as he was walking down the street, he was startled by a pigeon that flew up from beneath a bench right into his face. The shock was tremendous and he sat down on the bench to gather his wits and regain his breath, but found that he was panting heavily. His chest felt constricted and he couldn't seem to get enough air. He thought that he might suffocate and tried to breath faster, desperate to get some air, but only felt worse. A wave of panic rushed over him. Was he suffocating? Maybe he was having a heart attack. He was terrified that he was about to die. There were spots and lines in front of his eyes, and he didn't seem to be able to focus. He felt dizzy, and then had a sharp pain in his chest. He felt that he would pass out any second. It must be a heart attack. His terror increased. A worried passer-by called an ambulance for him, and they rushed him to Casualty. Later, at the hospital, he was told that he had suffered a panic attack.

The vicious cycle

Now that you've read Alex's story look at the diagram opposite. It shows how hyperventilation feeds into a vicious cycle of physical and mental symptoms. Fill in the boxes as if you were Alex.

Now let's take a closer look at your personal experience. You can use your personal records to help you complete the questions that follow.

What was the trigger?

_____

_____

_____

What was his physical response?

_____

_____

_____

How did that make Alex feel?

_____

_____

_____

What went through his mind?

_____

_____

_____

What sort of situations trigger rapid/shallow breathing in your case?

_____

_____

_____

What physical symptoms follow?

_____

_____

_____

What goes through your mind?

_____

_____

_____

How do this make you feel?

_____

_____

_____

Do you avoid anything as a result?

_____

_____

_____

The controlled breathing exercise

You can learn to correct hyperventilation and control the symptoms for yourself by practising how to breathe in a way which will counter it. This involves:

- breathing gently and evenly

- breathing through your nose

- breathing mainly from your diaphragm (the sheet of muscle between your lungs and stomach) rather than your upper chest/ribcage alone

- filling your lungs completely

- exhaling slowly and fully.

The controlled breathing exercise described below will help you develop this ability so that you can call on it when hyperventilation threatens. Aim to breathe smoothly, without any gulping or gasping.

1   Lie down. This will make it easier for you to feel the difference between shallow and deep breathing.

2   Place one hand on your chest and one on your stomach.

3   Breathe in through your nose, allowing your stomach to swell. This means that you are using your lungs fully.

4   Try to keep the movement in your upper chest/ribcage to a minimum and keep the overall movement gentle and smooth.

5   Slowly and evenly, breathe out through your nose.

6   Repeat steps 3–5. Each complete cycle counts as one breath, and you should aim to take between eight and twelve breaths a minute. This may be difficult to assess at first, so practise counting from slowly from 1 to 6 as you go through a complete cycle.

7   *Do not deep breathe rapidly*.

8   As you become more practised, try the exercise sitting or standing.

Breaking the cycle

CASE STUDY: Alex – Part 2

After his first panic attack, Alex was really sensitive to every bodily sensation – especially discomfort in his chest. When he had the first attack he was sure that the pain in his chest meant that he was having a heart attack. That fear stayed with him despite his doctor's assurances – while he felt fine in the clinic, he would start to panic again as soon as he felt an ache or a pain in his chest.

To help him get over his anxiety, Alex's doctor tried an experiment with him. After explaining about hyperventilation and how it works to create a vicious cycle of anxiety, he coached Alex in how to breathe slowly and evenly, from the diaphragm rather than the ribcage. Then he told him to start panting (overbreathing). Within seconds, Alex started to get chest pain and dizziness just like his 'heart attacks'. As soon as this started, the doctor talked him through the steps for controlled breathing, and Alex's dizziness and chest pain

faded. They repeated the experiment and Alex found that he was able to switch the symp-
toms on and off.

After that he was more confident and found that, whenever he got anxious, the con-
trolled breathing exercise would alleviate the symptoms, he would be able to assure
himself that he was well and this would calm him down. He followed the doctor's advice
to practise slow breathing during the day so that it would become a habit. Every time he
went to the bathroom, where he could have some privacy, Alex would spend two or three
minutes doing his breathing exercises.

Alex's case shows how a simple controlled breathing exercise can help you to break
every link in the hyperventilation cycle.

1 Restoring correct breathing calmed the physical symptoms he felt.

2 The exercise reassured him that he was only suffering from hyperventilation and
not a heart attack.

3 It made him feel in control rather than out-of-control and panicky.

Difficulties when learning controlled breathing

There are two main problems you may face with the controlled breathing exercise:

1 difficulty in breathing naturally and

2 forgetting to practise.

Difficulty in breathing naturally

When you first start practising the breathing exercise you may feel that you are not
getting enough air with each breath (which may encourage you to breathe too fast).
With practice you will find that the slower rate of breathing is comfortable, but you
will have to allow yourself time to get used to it.

● A good tip is to begin the exercise by breathing out as fully as you can. This helps
to empty your lungs as much as possible, so that the in-breath will be deeper and
easier.

Forgetting to practise

The eventual aim is for controlled breathing to become a habit, so that you no longer have to focus consciously on your breathing to know that you are doing it properly. For controlled breathing to become a habit, you need repeated rehearsal, so it is important to practise the exercise whenever you can.

- A good tip is to put a coloured spot (perhaps a child's sticker) somewhere eye-catching to remind you to use correct breathing each time you see it.

- You might find it useful to put the marker on your watch, as most of us look at our watches very regularly throughout the day.

As your skill improves, you will find it easier and easier to switch to a helpful style of breathing whenever you feel anxious. As with all anxiety management techniques, you will be most successful if you tackle your stress when it is at a low level. In other words, don't wait until you're in a panic to practise your breathing: get used to catching the signs of overbreathing early.

Summary

1 Hyperventilation is a natural response to exercise and stress.

2 It can become a problem if it is continuous, or inappropriate, causing distressing physical symptoms that trigger a vicious cycle of physical and psychological anxiety.

3 You can break this cycle and cope with hyperventilation by learning a simple controlled breathing exercise.

4 The most important points are to breathe slowly and deeply through your nose, using your diaphragm and not your ribcage (that is from the abdomen, not the upper chest).

5 You need to practise the technique for it to become effective.

SECTION 4: Relaxation Techniques

Another major physical symptom of stress and anxiety is muscular tension. This in turn can cause unpleasant physical and mental effects. Sometimes the physical stress reaction is just at the moment of high anxiety (churning stomach before an exam, for example) and sometimes the tension is ongoing (chronic headaches or back pain). Work through the checklist below and tick any symptoms that you have experienced when you were anxious.

Symptoms:

☐ Headache

☐ Stiff neck

☐ Painful shoulders

☐ Tight chest

☐ Breathing difficulty

☐ Trembling

☐ Churning stomach

☐ Difficulty in swallowing

☐ Blurred vision

☐ Back pain

Whether in the moment or chronic, the unpleasant sensations of muscular tension can trigger more tension. It can trigger worrying thoughts such as 'This will never get better' or 'I will never get a good night's sleep' or 'My stomach is churning so much I will have an accident'. In addition the pain and discomfort of physical tensions can promote more tension – think how tense we become if we have toothache. Thus, a vicious cycle of increasing tension is set up. A most effective way of controlling bodily tension is learning how to relax.

The relaxation programme

In this section you will be introduced to 'applied relaxation'. Applied relaxation means developing relaxation as a skill, so that you can reduce physical tension whenever you need to. Once you have mastered this skill you will be able to relieve tension in a variety of situations. When your body is free of tension, your mind will become more relaxed as well.

You can gain the ability to relax at will by working through the four structured exercises which follow. These make up a programme that is designed to help you learn to relax, step by step. The first two routines are quite long and you may find that taped instructions are helpful. You can make your own tape following the relaxation script (see pages 65–68), being sure to use slow, gentle speech.

The four stages are:

1 Progressive relaxation (PR)

2 Shortened PR

3 Simple relaxation

4 Cued relaxation

General guidelines for relaxing

● Plan when you will practise, and try to keep to this time each day so that you develop a routine which you will be able to stick to.

Think about your typical day. Now list two or three times during the day that would be suitable for practising a twenty-minute relaxation exercise:

Approx. time:

1 _____

2 _____

3 _____

- Practise the relaxation routine two or three times a day: the more you practise the more easily you will be able to relax.

- Make sure that you choose somewhere quiet to practise, and that no one will disturb you during your relaxation exercises.

Make a list here of possible places where you could practise relaxation.

_____

_____

_____

_____

_____

_____

_____

_____

_____

_____

- Do not try the exercise if you are hungry or have just eaten; or if the room is too hot or too chilly. This will make it difficult to relax.

- Start the exercise by lying down in a comfortable position, wearing comfortable clothes. Later, you can also practise relaxation while you are sitting or standing.

- Try to adopt a 'passive attitude', which means not worrying about your performance or whether you are successfully relaxing. Just 'have a go' and let it happen.

- *Breathing* is important: try to breathe through your nose, filling your lungs completely so that you feel your stomach muscles stretch. Breathe slowly and regularly. It is important that you do not take a lot of quick, deep breaths as this can make you feel dizzy or faint and even make your tension worse. If you place your hands on your stomach, you will feel movement if you are breathing properly. Try this out before you exercise to make sure that you are used to the feeling.

● Record your progress so that you can assess if the relaxation procedure is working for you. Use the record sheet opposite to keep details of your experiences. Expect day-to-day differences in your ability to relax – we all have days when relaxation comes easily and other days when it is more difficult.

Using the record sheet

Record your level of relaxation before and after each exercise, using the following scale:

1	2	3	4	5	6	7	8	9	10
Not relaxed, tense			Moderate relaxation				Completely relaxed		

Also note any relevant information, such as the sort of day you are having, where you are, things on your mind, etc. Use your record to check your progress and to discover where and when you are best able to relax.

Date/time	Rating before	Which exercise did you use?	Rating afterwards	Notes

Working through the exercises

For each exercise, read the instructions and familiarize yourself with the technique before you try it out. You will not be able to relax if you have to read the instructions at the same time.

When you are able to relax using the first exercise, move on to exercise two; when you have mastered this, begin exercise three. Finally, learn exercise four, which is a rapid relaxation routine. This whole process should be done gradually, over several weeks. The length of time needed will vary from person to person, so don't worry that you are not progressing 'fast enough' as this will reduce your ability to relax. Only move to the next exercise when you feel fully relaxed at the end of a routine: there is nothing to be gained by rushing through the programme.

Progressive relaxation (PR)

PR is a series of tense–relax exercises focusing on the body's major muscle groups. As well as helping you to relax, this technique teaches you to distinguish between tense and relaxed muscles. In this way you will learn to recognize when you are tense and need to relax.

The basic movement

You will perform a basic tense–relax movement for each of the muscle groups in your body. The basic movement is:

1 Tense the muscle (by following the instructions for that muscle group), but do not strain.

2 Concentrate on the sensation of tension; hold it for five seconds.

3 Relax the tension.

4 For ten to fifteen seconds, focus on how the muscle feels when it is relaxed.

The exercise

- Choose a quiet, comfortable, relaxing environment where you can lie down (for example on your bed).

- Breathe slowly and regularly during the exercise and between each stage in the procedure.

- Work through the following sequence:

Feet – Pull your toes back; tense the muscles in your feet. Relax and repeat.

Legs – Straighten your legs; point your toes towards your face. Relax; let your legs go limp; repeat.

Abdomen – Tense your stomach muscles by pulling them in and up – as if preparing to receive a punch. Relax and repeat.

Back – Arch your back. Relax and repeat.

Shoulders/neck – Shrug your shoulders as hard as you can, bringing them up and in. Press your head back. Relax and repeat.

Arms – Stretch out your arms and hands. Relax; let your arms hang limp; repeat.

Face – Tense your forehead and jaw. Lower your eyebrows and bite hard. Relax and repeat.

Whole body – Tense your entire body: feet, legs, abdomen, back, shoulders and neck, arms, and face. Hold the tension for a few seconds. Relax and repeat.

- If you still feel tense when you reach the end of the routine, go through it again.

- If only parts of your body feel tense, repeat the exercise in those areas.

- When you have finished the exercise and feel relaxed, spend a few moments relaxing your mind. Think about something restful: whatever scene or image works best for you.

- Breathe slowly through your nose, filling your lungs completely. Continue for a minute or two, then open your eyes.

- Do not stand up straight away; when you are ready, move *slowly* and stretch *gently*.

Mastering PR

Practise twice a day until you always feel fully relaxed at the end of the exercise. Then you can move on to shortened version. Remember, it takes time to learn how to relax. Give yourself a chance and do not expect to succeed too soon.

Shortened PR

Shorten your routine by missing out the 'tense' stage for each muscle group. Simply go through the sequence of relaxing the different muscle groups. When you can do this effectively, you can adapt the routine to use at other times and in other places. For example you could try the exercise sitting rather than lying down; or you might move from a quiet bedroom to the living area which is not so peaceful. In this way, you will be learning to relax in a range of environments which is what you need for real-life coping.

Simple relaxation

This is an even shorter exercise which you can practise as you become more experienced at achieving the relaxed state. Simple relaxation involves an element of meditation/visualization. It centres on using a relaxing word, sound or image as a focus.

Finding a relaxing word, sound or image

Exactly what you use is up to you. Answer the following questions to help you come up with ideas.

a Write down a word you find particularly calming or restful, either because of its sound or because of what it makes you think about. (For example, 'calm', 'home', 'peace' or 'sea'):

_____

b Write down a sound you find particularly calming or restful, either because of the noise or because of what it makes you think about (for example, the sound of waves on a beach or the wind in the trees):

_____

c Write down an object in your home that you find particularly calming or restful, either because of its shape/form/colour or because of what it makes you think about. (This might be an ornament or a favourite picture or photo):

_____

d Write down a mental image or scene that you find particularly calming or restful, either because of its visual properties or because of what it makes you think about. (For example, a sunlit meadow or a deserted beach):

_____

Try the exercise below with each of your four choices in turn. After each trial, record your impressions on the relaxation record sheet (see pages 34–35). When you've worked through all four of your options, compare your notes and ratings and choose the one that helps you to relax most effectively. Don't worry if you find that you need to do this exercise again in order to find something that works for you. This is often a process of trial and error but it is worth investing the time to find _your_ best solution.

The exercise

1 Sit in a comfortable position with your eyes closed. Imagine your body growing heavier and more relaxed.

2 Breathe in through your nose. As you inhale, focus on breathing correctly.

3 As you breathe out, start thinking about your relaxing word, sound or image.

4 Continue think about this while still breathing easily and naturally.

5 Don't worry whether or not you are good at the exercise; simply let go of your tensions and relax at your own pace. Distracting thoughts will probably come into your mind. Don't worry about this – just don't dwell on them. Return to your relaxing word, sound or image.

6 Keep going for as long as it takes you to feel relaxed. This might be two minutes or twenty minutes. Finish when you feel relaxed.

7 When you stop, sit quietly with your eyes closed for a few moments

8 Then sit with your eyes open. Don't stand up or begin moving around too quickly.

As this is a brief exercise, you can practise it more frequently than the earlier ones. Practise for a few minutes every hour; or at coffee, lunch and tea breaks; or between appointments; or at every service station if you are driving on a long journey and feeling stressed. The options are endless and the most useful thing you can do is to discover what fits in best with your lifestyle. Read Helen's story below to learn how Simple Relaxation helped her manage her health worries.

CASE STUDY: Helen

'I had to find a few minutes each day, at regular intervals, to sit and concentrate on breathing calmly and then imagining a soothing scene. My first choice didn't work too well – it was a tropical beach and I thought of myself lying in the sun, listening to the sea. I'm such an active person that this quickly began to irritate me! My next choice did work. I remembered a formal garden that we had visited earlier in the year and which I'd loved. So, in my mind, I went for a stroll around this garden, noticing all the different trees, shrubs and flowers and imagining the scent of the roses and the feel of the sun on my shoulders. I managed to find a postcard of the garden which helped make my mental picture more vivid.

'I did this exercise three or four times a day – whenever I got to the end of one chore and before I began the next. It was wonderful. No physical pains to worry me and I found that I had more energy if I relaxed during the day. Every now and then I get a twinge or an ache and I am alarmed, but I use this as my cue to relax and, so far, the discomfort has always gone away.'

Cued relaxation

When you are able to relax using the previous three exercises, you can start using your relaxation skills regularly throughout the day, and not simply at your 'specific' relaxation times. You will soon be able to relax 'at will' – this is what cued relaxation involves.

In cued relaxation you simply use a cue – something that will catch your attention and trigger your relaxation response – to remind you to:

1 Drop your shoulders

2 Relax the muscles in your body

3 Check that you are breathing correctly

4 Relax

Choosing a cue

You need to pick something that will catch your eye regularly throughout the day, wherever you are. As with the cue suggested for the breathing exercise (see page 29), a coloured dot in your wristwatch is a good idea. Try to think of something else you could use – work out what catches your eye frequently and use this as a reminder.

Applied relaxation

The final stage in relaxation training is being able to apply your skills whenever you need them – this is called 'applied relaxation'. With time and regular practice, relaxation will become a way of life and you will be able to relax at will. Of course you are bound to continue to experience some tension from time to time – this is normal – but you will now have better awareness of it and the skills to bring it under control.

Remember, to get to this point takes practice. You wouldn't be able to play the piano perfectly after one lesson – you need to build on separate skills, from practising scales to finger exercises. You'd then progress to playing simple tunes and finally something more complex.

Read Louise's story about how long it took her to learn relaxation methods.

CASE STUDY: Louise

'My counsellor explained that it would take time to get my anxiety under control and that she would first teach me how to relax my body and mind. I remember thinking that I had tried everything to relax. I told her that I'd hired romantic videos, I'd gone out to dinner with friends, I'd even joined an exercise class.

'Her method was different from my other relaxing activities because I did the exercise alone and focused on myself and the way I felt. It was quite difficult to get into at first, especially as the early exercises took fifteen to twenty minutes and they were a bit boring. As the exercises got shorter, I began to enjoy them more and I was more motivated to practise. However, I didn't think that it was going to take so long – I spent weeks learning to relax!

'Eventually, I reached the stage of being able to identify when I was tense and then I was able to drop my shoulders, regulate my breathing and empty my mind of worries. This is no mean feat, believe me. It was hard work and I nearly gave up several times, but now I'm glad I persevered because it has changed the way I feel. I am no longer dogged by that sense of doom and gloom because I can shake it off by relaxing whenever and wherever I need to.'

Difficulties in relaxing

Most people experience some problems during relaxation training. The most common ones are:

- Feeling strange
- Cramp
- Falling asleep
- Intruding/worrying thoughts
- Not feeling relaxed

Feeling strange

Any physical activity that you are not used to will feel strange at first. Don't worry about this as your tension will rise if you do. Try to accept that it will take a few practice sessions before you begin to feel comfortable with the exercises. After this you will find that the unusual sensations will soon disappear.

Unpleasant sensations can also be caused by overbreathing; getting up too soon after relaxing; and practising when you are too hungry or full. Make sure to rule these out before practising again.

Cramp

Cramp can be painful but is not dangerous.

- Use a warm room for your practice.
- Avoid tensing your muscles too hard.
- Ease cramp by rubbing the affected muscle; then resume your exercise gently.

Falling asleep

Sometimes this is what you will hope for, but if not, try doing the exercise sitting and not lying down. A handy tip is to hold something unbreakable in one hand (e.g. a plastic beaker), so that you will drop it if you nod off. This should help to keep you awake.

Intruding/worrying thoughts

These are quite normal. The best way of making sure that the thoughts go away is by not dwelling on them. Try to accept that they will drift into your mind from time to time and then simply refocus on your relaxation exercise. If you try *not* to think of the worrying thoughts they will not go away.

Not feeling relaxed

This can be a problem when you first begin relaxation training. When you are new to relaxation exercises you may not feel much benefit – this comes with practice. The most important thing is not to try too hard as this will create tension. Just let the sensations of relaxation happen when they happen. Also, check your environment (see 'General guidelines', above) – is it too warm/cold, noisy, busy, uncomfortable? Are you anxious that you might be disturbed?

Summary

1 Stress causes muscular tension, which in turn causes a range of unpleasant physical sensations.

2 These unpleasant feelings can be controlled by learning and practising a series of relaxation exercises: this takes time.

3 Eventually you can respond to physical tension by using relaxation to control the physical discomfort.

4 Physical relaxation can help your mind feel more calm.

SECTION 5: Managing Thoughts and Images

This section will help you to understand:

- How you can learn techniques that will distract you from anxious thoughts or images
- How you can learn to challenge anxiety-provoking thoughts

In Part One you learnt about the psychological symptoms of anxiety and how the thinking patterns triggered by anxiety can help to maintain and worsen that anxiety.

For example, if you were at a party and felt yourself blushing or not being able to speak easily, your thoughts could focus on how self-conscious and embarrassed you felt, which in turn would make you feel more anxious. If you had a slight chest pain and thought 'This could be a heart attack!', stress levels would rise and you would experience symptoms such as increased muscular tension, which would worsen the pain, and so the thoughts might become even more alarming: 'This *is* a heart attack!' The anxiety would get worse and a cycle of increasing tension would develop.

In this section you will learn two ways to break the cycle of anxious thoughts:

1 *distraction*, where you refocus your attention away from the anxiety-provoking thought or image, and

2 *challenging*, where you review your thinking and tackle unhelpful anxious-thoughts and images.

Distraction is dealt with here; challenging is covered on page 51.

Distraction

For most people it is possible to really concentrate on only one thing at once. When you turn your attention to something neutral or pleasant, you can distract yourself from worrying thoughts and images. By using specific techniques of distraction, you can break the cycle of worrying thoughts and prevent your anxiety increasing.

There are three basic distraction techniques which you can tailor to suit your needs. These are:

- *physical exercise*
- *refocusing*
- *mental exercise*

Successful distraction

The key to successful distraction lies in finding something that needs a great deal of attention, is very specific, and holds some interest for you. If a distraction task is too simple, too vague or too boring, it tends not to be effective. However, a distractor should not be so sophisticated or demanding that it becomes hard to engage with it.

Physical activity

This simply means keeping active when you are stressed. If you are physically occupied, you are less likely to be able to dwell on worrying thoughts or images. You could try taking exercise such as walking, jogging, playing squash, etc. These sorts of activities are particularly beneficial as they help use up the adrenaline, which can otherwise make you feel tense.

But activity doesn't just mean exercising – any type of physical task can do the trick. For instance, if you began to feel self-conscious at a party, you could offer to take drinks around to keep yourself busy and your mind off your anxieties. If your physical task requires mental effort, so much the better, because the distraction effect will be more powerful.

Different situations call for different activities. You could:

- play squash in the evening in order to work off the day's stress

- take a brief walk up and down the corridor when you are very tense at the office

- reorganize your desk when you are not able to leave the office but are alone

- unwind and rewind paper clips to take the edge off your anxiety in meetings.

Other distractions that you might try are taking the dog for a walk, reorganizing your garage or a room in the house if you are unable to go out, tidying your handbag, updating your diary if you are physically restricted in what you can do – in a doctor's waiting room, for example. See if you can suggest appropriate distracting physical activities for each of the following situations. Add your own if necessary.

Situation	Activity
A stressful day at the office	
Feeling tense before a meeting	

Situation	Activity
Worrying about your health or your family's	
Being at a party or social gathering	
Before an exam or test	
In a waiting room, waiting to see the doctor	

Refocusing

This means distracting yourself by paying close attention to things around you. If you were in a crowded street, you could try counting the number of men and women you could see with blonde hair, or look for certain objects in a shop window; in a café, you could listen to other people's conversations or study the details of a picture. You don't have to be sophisticated – you just need to find a range of activities that absorb your attention.

For example, if a woman were anxious about using the supermarket, she could read car number plates as her friend drove her to the store, attend closely to her shopping list while moving round the supermarket and, at the checkout, read the details on food packages, count the number of items in her own or another person's basket or browse through a magazine.

See if you can find objects to focus on during your particular anxiety-provoking situations.

Situation	Refocusing activity

Mental activity

This requires you to be more creative and to use more mental effort. You need to come up with a distracting phrase, picture or mental exercise for yourself. You might try singing a song to yourself, recalling a favourite holiday trip, practising mental arithmetic. Alternatively, study someone nearby and try to guess what they do, what interests they might have, where they are going and so on.

You could try dwelling on an imaginary scene to take your mind away from worrying thoughts. Make your scene come alive with colour and sounds and texture. For example you could:

- imagine your dream home and then walk through every room, studying the details

- recall a well-loved tune

- remember cycling over a familiar and much-loved track, paying attention to the scenery

- recall all the stages involved in making a complex flower display or redesigning your home.

The more detailed the mental tasks, the more distracting they are.

In the space below write down some of your own favourite scenes or memories, or images that you simply enjoy thinking about.

_____

_____

_____

_____

_____

_____

_____

_____

_____

Choosing the right distraction technique

- Before you use a distraction technique you must select one which is suited to you and the situation in which you need to be distracted. There is no point in dwelling on a picture of a sun-soaked beach if you hate the sea and you sunburn easily, or if your real love is skiing. In the same way, relying on physical activity to distract you might not be helpful if your anxiety attacks happen in social or interpersonal situations.

- Work out your preferences and needs and then tailor distraction to suit you. Try to make use of your own interests: if you are a keen gardener, you might use pruning and weeding as your physical activity; looking through the bus window at gardens and identifying plants as a refocusing exercise; and holding an image of a beautiful formal garden as a mental task.

- When you have established what you need, be creative in developing your own selection of distraction techniques. However, always be specific in your choice of task and choose exercises which demand much attention.

- When you have a collection of distraction techniques for different occasions, practise them whenever you have the chance. In this way, when you are stressed, you can switch your thoughts to your distraction quite easily.

Read Rita's story below for an example of how distraction helped her cope with her claustrophobia.

'I just can't bear enclosed spaces – theatres, churches, lifts, crowded shops. It really became a problem when my children, nieces and nephews were all getting married, having babies and then having them baptized. Suddenly, I was expected to go to church but I was terrified.

'Fortunately, I discovered a way of getting through the ceremonies. I taught myself ways of distracting my mind from my panicky thoughts if necessary. First, I always carried a really good book so that I could get lost in that if we had to sit around for too long. Second, I took my worry beads with me everywhere I went so that I could fiddle with them to take my mind off my worries. Finally, I taught myself a sort of meditation: I would be able to stand or sit, just like everyone else, but I imagined that I was somewhere else, somewhere safe. In my imagination I was back on the farm where I grew up and I could imagine walking through our fields with my father. Increasingly I found that I did not always have to resort to using the strategies as the knowledge that I could distract myself calmed me.'

Difficulties in using distraction

If your strategy does not work well, this could be because of the following.

- You are not practised enough. You need to practise more, especially when you are not anxious.

- The technique was not suited to the situation. Think what other strategies you have in your collection and give them a try.

- You were already too stressed to manage your anxiety effectively. Try to catch your anxiety earlier next time – any coping technique will work better if you are less stressed.

A final note

Many people find distraction very helpful in dealing with worries, fears and anxieties.

However, distraction does not suit everyone, and it can be unhelpful if you use it as a means of avoiding difficult situations. For example, if you were anxious about speaking with guests at social gatherings and you always distracted yourself by handing round the drinks, then you would never face your real fear and it would not go away. If this applies to you, you need to try a different means of thought management, called 'challenging'; this is described on the next page.

Summary

1 Worrying thoughts and images can trigger a cycle of increasing anxiety.

2 It is possible to distract yourself from the worries, and so break this cycle, by using the techniques of physical exercise; refocusing; and mental exercise.

3 These techniques have to be tailored to your needs and practised to be effective.

Challenging worrying thoughts and images

The technique of challenging requires you to do three things:

1 Identify your worrying thought or image

2 Ask yourself. 'Is this a realistic worry?' If it isn't a realistic concern, then

3 You need to replace it with a more helpful statement

You already know that anxiety causes us to think differently and that we can get caught up in a cycle of worry and increasing anxiety. Challenging is another way of interrupting the cycle by reducing the impact of the worrying thoughts.

Identifying anxious thoughts

This is the first step in challenging your worrying thoughts and images. Your best cue is feeling anxious. When you are aware of your tension rising, ask yourself: 'What is going through my mind?'

Types of anxious thoughts

Your worries may be in the form of sentences, such as 'I am going to make a fool of myself' or 'I think that I am having a heart attack', or in the form of a picture, such as a scene where you are losing control or an image of something terrible happening. It is not always easy to recognize worrying thoughts and images, but with practice you will become better able to identify what is going through your mind.

Keeping a thought diary

When you are feeling calm, it is not always easy to recall the thoughts or images that triggered your anxiety. Keeping a record of what goes through your mind near the time of the anxious episode can be the best way of discovering the words, images or phrases that cause your tension. Use the thought diary on page 57 as a daily record, writing down whatever is in your mind when you are anxious (there are blank thought diary sheets at the back of this Part). Column 1 asks you to note the date, time and situation relating to an anxious feeling. Column 2 asks you to catch the associated thought or image and to describe it in as much detail as possible. In column 3 you can use a rating out of 1 to 10 for the level of anxiety you felt: 0 would be no distress while 10 would be the worst that you could imagine.

In order to tease out the key thoughts, ask yourself questions such as: What went through my mind just then? What is so bad about that? What does this say about me or my future? How do I think others see me? What bad thing might happen?

Like other coping skills, recording anxious thoughts successfully takes practice. If you continue to find this exercise difficult, remember that timing is important: if you do not 'catch' a thought as it occurs, you may lose it. Also, try not to shy away from examining what you feel and think. Although in the short term you may feel upset by looking closely at your thoughts, in doing so you will eventually be able to take control of your worries and anxiety.

Questioning anxious thoughts

When you have recorded your stressful thoughts, you will need to see if they fall into any of the unhelpful ways of thinking we looked at in Part One, page 12. Here is a reminder of the main types of unhelpful thinking.

Catastrophizing: anticipating total disaster if something minor goes wrong.

All-or-nothing thinking: viewing things in 'either/or' terms and overlooking degree and compromise.

Exaggerating: magnifying negative or weak aspects, forgetting the positive aspects and the signs of your strengths.

Over-generalizing: deciding *everything* to be awful *always* because of one bad experience.

Ignoring the positive: overlooking personal strengths and good experiences and dwelling on the negative aspects of yourself and your life.

Scanning: searching for the thing you fear.

Worrying: getting caught up in a cycle of unproductive 'What if…'s.

At this stage you are trying to work out whether or not your thoughts are reasonable. At the time of feeling anxious or worried, you might not be able to be objective and to spot unhelpful thinking patterns or predictions. If that is the case, look at your record later, when you are feeling calm and more able to view the situation clearly.

If you still have difficulty ask a friend to look through your diary entries and to comment on how accurate they think your thoughts were. In Column 4 of the diary write down any types of negative thinking you can see at work as this should help you gain perspective.

Finding other ways of thinking

Now you can begin to find other ways of thinking that don't cause an unreasonable amount of anxiety. There are five questions you should ask yourself to develop a more confident way of thinking.

The Five Questions

1 *Are there reasons for my having this worrying thought?* This question will help you to understand why you have the worry and make it less likely that you feel silly or embarrassed about it.

2 *Are there reasons against my holding this thought?* This question helps you to look for evidence and experiences to undermine and weaken your anxiety. You could use a friend or a partner to help you find statements to challenge your worry. Ask yourself questions such as: Are there times that I did not feel like this? …and why? Are there times that I have dealt with this situation? …how? What would I say to myself if I were calm? How would my best friend view the situation?

3 *What is the worst thing that could happen?* Be brave and consider the worst outcome of the situation that bothers you. This is the nub of the fear that you are challenging.

4 *How could I cope with this?* Now work out a plan for coping in the worst situation. If you can cope with the worst thing that could happen, you can feel confident that you can manage your anxiety. Reflect on your own assets and skills and on your successful coping experiences in the past. Think about how you might change the problem situation or change how you feel about it. Also consider how others can help: what advice and support are available from family, friends or professionals? Again, you might find it helpful to get someone else's views on this.

5 *What is a more helpful way of viewing the situation?* Look back over the notes you have made and try to form a new realistic statement in response to your initial worry. You can then use this to complete column 5, 'How can I challenge this?', in your diary. In order to get a sense of how effective your challenge is, rerate your anxiety levels at this point (using column 6).

Challenging is a demanding technique, and when you first start to do this exercise you might find that it takes you some time and that you need to keep notes. Look at the case studies below to see how this strategy can be used. In each case asking the Five Questions helps challenge the worrying thought.

CASE STUDY: Challenging in Action

1: Anxieties about a Friend

Worrying thought: 'Sara is late for our meeting. She might have had a car crash and have been injured.'

1 *Are there reasons for my having this worrying thought?* Yes, there are: I read about people being killed in road accidents and she is travelling on a main road where she could have an accident. So I am not being completely ridiculous.

2 *Are there reasons against my holding this thought?* Yes, there are: plenty of people use that road day in and day out and never have an accident. The weather conditions today are very good for driving and so an accident is even less likely than usual. Even if Sara were in an accident, she need not be badly hurt – quite a few of my friends have had accidents and experienced very minor injuries, if any. There are road works on the road she uses – they could account for her being late.

3 *What is the worst thing that could happen?* The worst thing is that she's had an accident and is injured.

4 *How would I cope with this?* This would be a difficult situation for me, but I could get my husband to support me. We could contact the accident services at the hospital to find out how badly she'd been hurt. I would want to visit and could take my husband with me. I would tell myself that she will be well looked after in the hospital.

5 *What is a more helpful way of looking at the situation?* It is unlikely that Sara has had an accident and she's probably late because of road works. If she has had an accident, then she is not necessarily badly injured; and if she were, I could reassure myself that the hospital staff are the best people to deal with this and use my husband to support me if I am distressed.

CASE STUDY: Challenging in Action

2: Dealing with Physical Symptoms

Worrying thought: 'I feel dizzy and light-headed. I am beginning to sweat and feel sick. I am sure that I am going to pass out in this shop and make a fool of myself.'

1 *Are there reasons for my having this worrying thought?* Yes, there are: my friend works in a shop and says that customers frequently feel faint and sometimes pass out in public. I once fainted in church, so I know that it is possible.

2 *Are there reasons against my holding this thought?* Yes, there are: I have often felt like this when I have been anxious. I now know that symptoms of anxiety are like the sensations that I am experiencing now – and I know that worrying and over-breathing will make them worse.

3 *What is the worst thing that could happen?* The worst thing is that I would faint here in the shop and I would look foolish.

4 *How would I cope with this?* I could get myself to reception and find a chair and someone to help me if I needed help. Meanwhile, I can try to cope with the unpleasant feelings by practising my controlled breathing and brief relaxation exercises. If I did actually faint, someone would come to my rescue: my friend says that shop staff are always ready to deal with this kind of emergency.

5 *What is a more helpful way of looking at the situation?* It is very hot in here and that could have triggered these unpleasant feelings; my anxiety is probably making them worse and I know that I can control things by finding a quiet spot and using my anxiety management skills. Even if I fainted, I would recover and feel all right because I felt fine when I came round after I passed out in church. However, I was ill at that time and that is why I fainted – I am not ill now. My friend says that people do feel faint in large shops, so a staff member won't be surprised if I ask for help. I never think that someone is foolish if they feel unwell, so people are unlikely to think that I am.

CASE STUDY: Challenging in Action

3: Fear of Spiders

Worrying thought: 'It's a cobweb. That means a spider – I have to get out of the room.'

1 *Are there reasons for my having this worrying thought?* Yes! Cobwebs and spiders go together and I know that I can go to pieces if I see a spider.

2 *Are there reasons against my holding this thought?* Sometimes I have mistaken cracks and pieces of hair for cobwebs and I have recently had experiences of being able to cope with small spiders.

3 *What is the worst thing that could happen?* It could be a spider and I could become terrified and feel sick.

4 *How would I cope with this?* In the recent past, I have used controlled breathing and distraction which has helped me to calm down. I could also call Carl for support and, if the worst came to the worst, I could always run away.

5 *What is a more helpful way of looking at the situation?* This might or might not be a cobweb and that might or might not mean that there's a spider here. Even if there is a spider, it could be small enough for me to tolerate or I might be able to use some coping strategies to deal with the situation. Carl is only in the next room if I need him and even if he couldn't come to support me, I could simply leave this room – although that would be my last resort.

Thought Diary

1. Date/time/ situation	2. What was going through your mind?	3. Rating	4. Unhelpful way of thinking	5. How can I challenge this?	6. Rerating

Challenge your own thoughts

Now that you've had a chance to see how thought challenging works, try challenging some of your own anxious thoughts. Choose an anxious thought from your diary, or simply note down a typical thought of the type that makes you anxious, and then write down your answers to the Five Questions for that thought. This will give a wider perspective and will help you come up with a alternative, less frightening possibility for column 5.

My worrying thought 1:

_____

_____

_____

_____

1 *Are there reasons for my having this worrying thought?*

_____

_____

_____

2 *Are there reasons against my holding this thought?*

_____

_____

_____

3 *What is the worst thing that could happen?*

_____

_____

_____

4 *How would I cope with this?*

_____

_____

_____

5 *What is a more helpful way of looking at the situation? (Column 5)*

_____

_____

_____

My worrying thought 2:

_____

_____

_____

_____

1 *Are there reasons for my having this worrying thought?*

_____

_____

_____

2 *Are there reasons against my holding this thought?*

_____

_____

_____

3 *What is the worst thing that could happen?*

_____

_____

_____

4 *How would I cope with this?*

_____

_____

_____

5 *What is a more helpful way of looking at the situation? (Column 5)*

_____

_____

_____

My worrying thought 3:

_____

_____

_____

1 *Are there reasons for my having this worrying thought?*

_____

_____

_____

2 *Are there reasons against my holding this thought?*

_____

_____

_____

3 *What is the worst thing that could happen?*

_____

_____

_____

4 *How would I cope with this?*

_____

_____

_____

5 *What is a more helpful way of looking at the situation? (Column 5)*

_____

_____

_____

My worrying thought 4:

_____

_____

_____

_____

1 *Are there reasons for my having this worrying thought?*

_____

_____

_____

2 *Are there reasons against my holding this thought?*

_____

_____

_____

3 *What is the worst thing that could happen?*

_____

_____

_____

4 *How would I cope with this?*

_____

_____

_____

5 *What is a more constructive way of viewing the situation? (Column 5)*

_____

_____

_____

Difficulties in challenging

Can it be as simple as it seems?

The examples above might make thought challenging seem simple, but it's not necessarily easy. If it were, you would be doing it all the time and would not need this manual. Like any skill it takes practice, and practice should begin when you are not feeling anxious so that you can be as objective as possible.

Remember that it can also be difficult to challenge worrying thoughts when you are distressed. Don't be surprised if you have to start by keeping a thought diary (see page 51) and challenging your worries after you have calmed down. Eventually you will be able to challenge your thoughts in the anxiety-provoking situation itself, without needing the diary to help you structure your thinking.

'I can't hold on to my worrying thoughts'

Do write down your thoughts, because thought management is more effective if you clearly spell out your worries. Anxious thoughts often come in the form of questions, such as 'What is going to happen, will I pass out?' or 'Are they thinking that I look foolish?' It is difficult to argue with questions, so try turning them into statements. For example:

Question:

'What if something bad has happened?'

'What is going to happen, will I pass out?'

'What if I see a spider?'

'Are they thinking that I look foolish?'

Statement:

'I am worried that my friend has been injured in an accident.'

'I am worried that I will pass out.'

'I am worried that I will see a spider that is too large for me to cope with.'

'I am worried that they think that I look foolish.'

It is very likely that the same thought or the same types of thought will crop up again and again. This is an advantage – the more often a worry occurs, the more opportunity you have to think up ways to challenge it.

'I can't remember my challenging statements when I need them'

Make sure you write down your challenging statements in full. They will have more impact if you spell them out to yourself. The more you get into the habit of examining your worries thoroughly, the better you will be at thought challenging.

'It's taking too long to work'

If you keep at it you will find that rational responses to worrying thoughts or images become as automatic for you as your anxiety responses are now. But you should expect to have 'good' days and 'bad' days – this is normal. There are going to be times when you are unwell, tired or just too distressed to put thought challenging into action in a stressful situation. Don't worry about this too! Try to use distraction as a way of coping with the anxiety. When you are feeling calmer, think about helpful, rational responses to your worries. Also try to understand why challenging was difficult for you on this occasion.

Summary

1   Everyone has worrying thoughts and images and they only become a problem when they are not easily dismissed.

2   Worrying can develop into a cycle of increasing anxiety if exaggerated beliefs are not challenged.

3   With practice, you can challenge your worries. You can do this by asking yourself how real is your fear and then generating a helpful, rational statement in response to it.

Scripts for Relaxation Techniques

Although many discover that relaxation training is an invaluable exercise in stress management, some do find that it is difficult to remember all the elements of each exercise and to pace the exercises properly. If you find that this is so, you can make your own instruction tapes by recording the scripts below. The aim of making the tape is to provide you with soothing instructions, so choose a time when you are feeling reasonably relaxed and your voice is not strained and you are not hurried. If you prefer the sound of a friend's voice, ask her or him to make the tape for you.

Exercise 1: Progressive relaxation or deep relaxation

This exercise will help you to distinguish between tension and relaxation in your muscles, and teach you how to relax at will. You will work through various muscle groups, first tensing them and then relaxing them. You will start with your feet, then work up through your body slowly and smoothly. Don't rush, just let the sensation of relaxation deepen at its own pace.

First, get as comfortable as you can...Lie flat on the floor with a pillow under your head, or snuggle in your chair...If you wear glasses, remove them...Kick off your shoes and loosen any tight clothing...Relax your arms by your side and have your legs uncrossed. Close your eyes, and don't worry if they flicker – this is quite usual.

Instructions

'You are beginning to relax...Breathe out slowly...Now, breathe in smoothly and deeply...Now breathe out slowly again, imagining yourself becoming heavier and heavier, sinking into the floor or your chair...Keep breathing rhythmically, and feel a sense of relief and letting go...Try saying "relax" to yourself as you breathe out ...Breathe like this for a few moments more...

(Read once)

'Now, begin to tense and relax the muscles of your body...Think of your feet...Tense the muscles in your feet and ankles, curling your toes towards your head...Gently stretch your muscles...Feel the tension in your feet and ankles...Hold it...Now let go...Let your feet go limp and floppy...Feel the difference...Feel the tension draining away from your feet...Let your feet roll outwards and grow heavier and heavier...Imagine that they are so heavy that they are sinking into the floor...More and more relaxed...growing heavier and more relaxed...

(Repeat)

'Now think about your calves...Begin to tense the muscles in your lower legs...If you are sitting, lift your legs up and hold them in front of you, feeling the tension ...Gently stretch the muscles...Feel the tension...Hold it...Now release...Let your feet touch the floor and let your legs go floppy and heavy...Feel the difference...Feel the tension leaving your legs, draining away from your calves...Leaving your calves feeling heavy...Draining away from your feet...Leaving them feeling heavy and limp...Imagine that your legs and feet are so heavy that they are sinking into the floor...They feel limp and relaxed...Growing more and more heavy and relaxed...

(Repeat)

'Think about your thigh muscles...Tense them by pushing the tops of your legs together as hard as you can...Feel the tension building...Hold it...Now, let your legs fall apart...Feel the difference...Feel the tension draining away from your legs ...They feel limp and heavy...Your feet feel heavy...Imagine the tension draining away...Leaving your legs...Leaving them feeling limp and relaxed...Leaving them feeling so heavy that they are sinking into the floor or your chair...Let the feeling of relaxation spread up from your feet...Up through your legs...Relaxing your hips and lower back...

(Repeat)

'Now tense the muscles of your hips and lower back by squeezing your buttocks together...Arch your back, gently...Feel the tension...Hold the tension...Now let it go...Let your muscles relax...Feel your spine supported again...Feel the muscles relax...Deeper and deeper...More and more relaxed...Growing heavier and heavier...Your hips are relaxed...Your legs are relaxed...Your feet are heavy ...Tension is draining away from your body...

(Repeat)

'Tense your stomach and chest muscles, imagine that your are expecting a punch in the stomach and prepare yourself for the impact...Take in a breath, and as you do, pull in your stomach and feel the muscles tighten...Feel your chest muscles tighten and become rigid...Hold the tension...Now slowly breathe out and let go of the tension...Feel your stomach muscles relax...Feel the tightness leave your chest... As you breathe evenly and calmly, your chest and stomach should gently rise and fall ...Allow your breathing to become rhythmic and relaxed...

(Repeat)

'Now think about your hands and arms…Slowly curl your fingers into two tight fists …Feel the tension…Now hold your arms straight out in front of you, still clenching your fists…Feel the tension in your hands, your forearms and your upper arms… Hold it…Now, let go…Gently drop your arms by your side and imagine the tension and imagine the tension draining away from your arms…Leaving your upper arms …Leaving your forearms…Draining away from your hands…Your arms feel heavy and floppy…Your arms feel limp and relaxed…

(Repeat)

'Think about the muscles in your shoulders…Tense them by drawing up your shoulders towards your ears and pull them in towards your spine…Feel the tension across your shoulders and in your neck…Tense the muscles in your neck further by tipping your head back slightly…Hold the tension…Now relax…Let your head drop forward…Let your shoulders drop…Let them drop even further…Feel the tension easing away from your neck and shoulders…Feel your muscles relaxing more and more deeply…Your neck is limp and your shoulders feel heavy…

(Repeat)

'Think about your face muscles…Focus on the muscles running across your forehead…Tense them by frowning as hard as you can…Hold that tension and focus on your jaw muscles…Tense the muscles by biting hard…Feel your jaw muscles tighten…Feel the tension in your face…Across your forehead…Behind your eyes …In your jaw…Now let go…Relax your forehead and drop your jaw…Feel the strain easing…Feel the tension draining away from your face…Your forehead feels smooth and relaxed…Your jaw is heavy and loose…Imagine the tension leaving your face…Leaving your neck…Draining from your shoulders…Your head, neck and shoulders feel heavy and relaxed.

(Repeat)

'Think of your whole body now…Your entire body feels heavy and relaxed…Let go of any tension…Imagine the tension flowing out of your body…Listen to the sound of your calm, even breathing…Your arms, legs and head feel pleasantly heavy…Too heavy to move…You may feel as though you are floating…Let it happen…It is part of being relaxed…

'When images drift into your mind, don't fight them…Just acknowledge them and let them pass…You are a bystander: interested but not involved…Enjoy the feeling of relaxation for a few more moments…If you like, picture something which gives you pleasure and a sense of calm…

'In a moment, I will count backwards from four to one…When I reach one, open your eyes and lie still for a little while before you begin to move around again…You will feel pleasantly relaxed and refreshed…

'Four: beginning to feel more alert…Three: getting ready to start moving again …Two: aware of your surroundings…One: eyes open, feeling relaxed and alert.'

Exercise 2: Simple relaxation routine

You can use a shorter exercise, which you can practise at almost any time you need to. For the shorter routine, you have to imagine a mental image or mental device to use during the relaxation exercise. This can be a pleasant, calming scene, such as a deserted beach; a particularly relaxing picture or object; or sound or word, which you find soothing, like the sound of the sea or the word 'serene'. The important thing is that you should find a mental device, which is calming for you

From time to time, distracting thoughts will come into your mind – this is quite usual. Don't dwell on them, simply return to thinking about your soothing image or sound. Once you have started the exercise, carry on for 10 to 20 minutes and, when you have finished, sit quietly with your eyes closed for a few moments. When you open your eyes, don't begin moving around too quickly.

To start the exercise, sit in a comfortable position. First, focus on your breathing. Take a slow, deep breath in…Feel the muscle beneath your rib cage move…Now let it out – slowly…Aim for a smooth pattern of breathing.

Instructions

'Close your eyes, and while you continue to breathe slowly, imagine your body becoming more heavy…Scan your body for tension…Start at your feet and move up through your body to your shoulders and head…If you find any tension, try to relax that part of your body…Now, while your body is feeling as heavy and comfortable as possible, become aware of your breathing again…Breathe in through your nose, and fill your lungs fully…Now, breathe out again and bring to mind your tranquil image or sound…Breathe easily and naturally as you do this…Again, breathe in through your nose, filling your lungs…and out, thinking of your soothing mental device…When you are ready to breathe in again, repeat the cycle…Keep repeating this cycle until you feel relaxed and calm and refreshed.

'When you have finished this exercise, sit quietly for a few moments, and enjoy the feeling of relaxation.'

Extra Charts and Worksheets

DIARY:

Monitor your stress levels each day, noting when you feel particularly worried, frightened or anxious. Use the diary as near to the time of distress as possible as it is easy to forget the details later. Record the occasion and rate the severity of your feelings (1–10). Where you can, note what triggered the stress – thoughts, images, feelings, events, for example. Also, record how you tried to cope, and afterwards, rerate your distress levels.

Rate your distress on the following scale:

1	2	3	4	5	6	7	8	9	10
No distress, calm				Moderate distress					Absolute panic

Date/time	What was the occasion?	Rating	What brought it on?	How did you try to cope?	Rerating

DIARY:

Monitor your stress levels each day, noting when you feel particularly worried, frightened or anxious. Use the diary as near to the time of distress as possible as it is easy to forget the details later. Record the occasion and rate the severity of your feelings (1–10). Where you can, note what triggered the stress – thoughts, images, feelings, events, for example. Also, record how you tried to cope, and afterwards, rerate your distress levels.

Rate your distress on the following scale:

1	2	3	4	5	6	7	8	9	10
No distress, calm				Moderate distress					Absolute panic

Date/time	What was the occasion?	Rating	What brought it on?	How did you try to cope?	Rerating

DIARY:

Monitor your stress levels each day, noting when you feel particularly worried, frightened or anxious. Use the diary as near to the time of distress as possible as it is easy to forget the details later. Record the occasion and rate the severity of your feelings (1–10). Where you can, note what triggered the stress – thoughts, images, feelings, events, for example. Also, record how you tried to cope, and afterwards, rerate your distress levels.

Rate your distress on the following scale:

1	2	3	4	5	6	7	8	9	10
No distress, calm				Moderate distress					Absolute panic

Date/time	What was the occasion?	Rating	What brought it on?	How did you try to cope?	Rerating

DIARY:

Monitor your stress levels each day, noting when you feel particularly worried, frightened or anxious. Use the diary as near to the time of distress as possible as it is easy to forget the details later. Record the occasion and rate the severity of your feelings (1–10). Where you can, note what triggered the stress – thoughts, images, feelings, events, for example. Also, record how you tried to cope, and afterwards, rerate your distress levels.

Rate your distress on the following scale:

1	2	3	4	5	6	7	8	9	10
No distress, calm				Moderate distress					Absolute panic

Date/time	What was the occasion?	Rating	What brought it on?	How did you try to cope?	Rerating

DIARY:

Monitor your stress levels each day, noting when you feel particularly worried, frightened or anxious. Use the diary as near to the time of distress as possible as it is easy to forget the details later. Record the occasion and rate the severity of your feelings (1–10). Where you can, note what triggered the stress – thoughts, images, feelings, events, for example. Also, record how you tried to cope, and afterwards, rerate your distress levels.

Rate your distress on the following scale:

1	2	3	4	5	6	7	8	9	10
No distress, calm				Moderate distress				Absolute panic	

Date/time	What was the occasion?	Rating	What brought it on?	How did you try to cope?	Rerating

DIARY:

Monitor your stress levels each day, noting when you feel particularly worried, frightened or anxious. Use the diary as near to the time of distress as possible as it is easy to forget the details later. Record the occasion and rate the severity of your feelings (1–10). Where you can, note what triggered the stress – thoughts, images, feelings, events, for example. Also, record how you tried to cope, and afterwards, rerate your distress levels.

Rate your distress on the following scale:

1	2	3	4	5	6	7	8	9	10
No distress, calm				Moderate distress					Absolute panic

Date/time	What was the occasion?	Rating	What brought it on?	How did you try to cope?	Rerating

DIARY:

Monitor your stress levels each day, noting when you feel particularly worried, frightened or anxious. Use the diary as near to the time of distress as possible as it is easy to forget the details later. Record the occasion and rate the severity of your feelings (1–10). Where you can, note what triggered the stress – thoughts, images, feelings, events, for example. Also, record how you tried to cope, and afterwards, rerate your distress levels.

Rate your distress on the following scale:

1	2	3	4	5	6	7	8	9	10
No distress, calm				Moderate distress					Absolute panic

Date/time	What was the occasion?	Rating	What brought it on?	How did you try to cope?	Rerating

DIARY:

Monitor your stress levels each day, noting when you feel particularly worried, frightened or anxious. Use the diary as near to the time of distress as possible as it is easy to forget the details later. Record the occasion and rate the severity of your feelings (1–10). Where you can, note what triggered the stress – thoughts, images, feelings, events, for example. Also, record how you tried to cope, and afterwards, rerate your distress levels.

Rate your distress on the following scale:

1	2	3	4	5	6	7	8	9	10
No distress, calm				Moderate distress					Absolute panic

Date/time	What was the occasion?	Rating	What brought it on?	How did you try to cope?	Rerating

78

Thought Diary

1. Date/time/ situation	2. What was going through your mind?	3. Rating	4. Unhelpful way of thinking	5. How can I challenge this?	6. Rerating

Thought Diary

1. Date/time/ situation	2. What was going through your mind?	3. Rating	4. Unhelpful way of thinking	5. How can I challenge this?	6. Rerating

Thought Diary

1. Date/time/situation	2. What was going through your mind?	3. Rating	4. Unhelpful way of thinking	5. How can I challenge this?	6. Rerating

Thought Diary

1. Date/time/ situation	2. What was going through your mind?	3. Rating	4. Unhelpful way of thinking	5. How can I challenge this?	6. Rerating

82

Thought Diary

1. Date/time/ situation	2. What was going through your mind?	3. Rating	4. Unhelpful way of thinking	5. How can I challenge this?	6. Rerating

Thought Diary

1. Date/time/ situation	2. What was going through your mind?	3. Rating	4. Unhelpful way of thinking	5. How can I challenge this?	6. Rerating

84

Thought Diary

1. Date/time/ situation	2. What was going through your mind?	3. Rating	4. Unhelpful way of thinking	5. How can I challenge this?	6. Rerating

Thought Diary

1. Date/time/ situation	2. What was going through your mind?	3. Rating	4. Unhelpful way of thinking	5. How can I challenge this?	6. Rerating

Thought Diary

1. Date/time/ situation	2. What was going through your mind?	3. Rating	4. Unhelpful way of thinking	5. How can I challenge this?	6. Rerating